The 7-Day Sex Challenge

Turn up the heat and
deepen the love
in your marriage!

by Jim and Carrie Gordon

This book is dedicated to:

…the spouse courageous enough to buy this book—and to their partner courageous enough to read it with them

…the couple who bought this book out of curiosity

…the couple who bought this book wanting to put the spark back in their marriage

…the couple hoping to revive a struggling relationship

…and to those couples who finish all seven days of the challenge!

CONTENTS

Part 2: The Challenge!

ACKNOWLEDGMENTS

Thanks to our publishing team: Joshua Gordon, Laurie MacNevin, and Michael Gordon.

Josh, you've always believed in our work to help marriages. Your support as Project Manager is what moved us from an idea to project completion!

Laurie, your contribution as Book Editor proved to us just how good you are at what you do! Your expert suggestions helped us more clearly communicate an important message to couples.

Michael, your cover design fits perfectly with the 7-Day Sex Challenge book title! The graphic design is intriguing, sensitive, and communicates fun!

Thanks to our website readers: it is an honour to come alongside you on your journey toward a great marriage!

Thanks to our Lord and Saviour, Jesus Christ. He has enriched us with the wonderful gift of marriage! His sacrificial love for us is the best example to follow in our marriages.

WHAT IS THE 7-DAY SEX CHALLENGE?

The 7-Day Sex Challenge is exactly what it sounds like: for seven days in a row you and your spouse will have sex. But you won't just be having sex. For seven days you'll be talking together, asking each other questions, trying new things, and learning more about one another than you ever knew before.

This challenge is designed to breathe new life into your marriage and help you reach new levels of intimacy with your spouse. We're so glad you've decided to commit to this challenge!

No matter how wonderful or how disappointing your relationship is right now, there's always room for improvement!

To improve and reach the next level of intimacy, joy, and sexual fulfillment you will gain new insights, be equipped with new relationship skills, and develop new habits. This is what the *7-Day Sex Challenge* is all about!

How to Use This Book

For each day of the challenge you will have four objectives. They are as follows:

1. Husband and wife will each read their segment of the "Statement of Biblical Design for Marriage".

2. Husband and wife will read a version of the standard marriage vows aloud to one another.

3. You will take time to enjoy sex with one another. Sex means that both husband and wife experience orgasm, though not necessarily simultaneously. We have also included some suggestions for you to use to add spice during the week's lovemaking.

4. Lastly, each of you will keep a personal journal where you comment on your experience and your progress throughout the

seven days.

You'll find all of the *7-Day Sex Challenge* resources organized in the next few sections:

Part 1: Getting Ready

Use these resources before Day One:

- Sex Challenge Commitment Form
- Intimacy Survey
- Intimacy Questions to Ask Your Partner
- Sex Challenge Pre-Reading

Part 2: The Challenge!

These resources will be used daily from Day One to Day Seven:

- Statement of Biblical Design for Marriage
- Marriage Vows
- Sex Challenge Journal

Part 1

Getting Ready

LET'S GET READY!

The following four steps are to be done before the first day of the *7-Day Sex Challenge*. These prerequisites are best spread out over several days, so don't try to do them all in one shot!

1. **Intimacy Commitment** (page 11)
    The first step is your actual decision to do the challenge. We have a form for you and your spouse to sign together.

2. **Intimacy Survey** (page 17)
    Each partner will complete an Intimacy Survey. Share and discuss your survey answers with one another.

9

3. **Intimacy Questions** (page 25)
   Plan a date night where the two of you can get away and ask one another a series of questions related to sexual intimacy in your relationship.

4. **Sex Challenge Pre-Reading** (page 29)
   The background reading is critical for success in this challenge. We have articles for you to read together as we work through six important concepts. The six concepts are:
   - The Truth about Commitment
   - The Truth about Forgiveness
   - The Truth about Design
   - The Truth about Vows
   - The Truth about Rewinding
   - The Truth about Sex

Your Commitment to Intimacy

During the next seven days, it's important that both of you climax during love-making. Both husbandband and wife need to enjoy sexual fulfillment together, regularly. Sex and the experience of orgasm are not just designed for men. As we examine female physiology, we discover women are "wired" to experience *greater* sexual potential than men!

Almost 10,000 husbands and wives have completed the online Intimacy Survey found on our website. The results indicate that many wives rarely experience orgasm; part of the issue may relate to the need for more *time* for women to climax. During this seven day course, it is important that both husband and wife climax; this encourages both of you to invest the necessary time to enjoy lovemaking together. Husbands, if your wife has difficulty reaching orgasm or it happens infrequently, then use this *7-Day Sex Challenge* as an investment of time to more diligently work at learning how your wife's body responds. Then, after the course, do whatever it takes to adjust your busy lifestyle so that there is regularly enough time during love-making to bring your wife to climax.

You may be tempted on a day when you're running out of time, to forgo mutual lovemaking and resort to the popular "quickie". Consider this: a simple-minded analogy relates to fast food vs. a home-cooked meal. Fast food takes less time and is okay to eat occasionally. The best lifestyle, though, is built around the option that takes more time but is much better for you in the long run! In the same way, an occasional quickie for the husband is great but this must not replace mutual love-making with both partners climaxing.

Sex Challenge Commitment Form

Read the following form together and sign it. By doing so, you are giving your spouse permission to use this form, if necessary, in the next week to remind you of your promise!

7-Day Sex Challenge Commitment

This confirms that

_____ and _____
husband   wife

have taken up the 7-Day Sex Challenge

for each of the next seven days beginning

_____,
date

We will:

• Read the Statement of Biblical Design for Marriage aloud to one another daily

• Read our portions of the Marriage Vows aloud to our spouse daily

• Endeavor to implement the truth of these words we have spoken each day, and ask God to make them more real to us

• Keep a daily journal to record our progress, thoughts, and feelings

14

• Engage in sex with one another, investing in at least twenty to thirty minutes of foreplay

• Ask one another what we might do to please each other sexually

• Bring one another to climax

• Cuddle and enjoy the afterglow!

Free from distraction, we will join together, at mutually agreed upon times, in the above marriage enriching activities. The purpose is to learn to love each other better, and to become as emotionally close to one another as possible!

We will complete all of the activities, each day, and record our progress.

Signatures:

Husband _____

Wife _____

INTIMACY SURVEYS

Before you even begin the *7-Day Sex Challenge*, each of you will complete your own Intimacy Survey. After completing the surveys, discuss your responses with your spouse. Use the survey as a safe forum for the two of you to share more openly and vulnerably than ever before.

Thank your spouse for their honesty! Even though your spouse's survey responses may trigger negative emotions, stay open and willing to listen. Remember, you are both on the same side of this challenge. Agree that this *7-Day Sex Challenge* will help your sexual relationship improve!

HIS INTIMACY SURVEY

Check all of the following statements that apply to you:

☐ My wife and I are comfortable talking about sex.

☐ We laugh and have fun during sex.

☐ My wife and I know where to find the female g-spot.

☐ Our sex life has improved in the past year.

☐ My wife and I kiss more now than in our first year of marriage.

☐ I initiate sex at least 25% of the time.

☐ We try to include variety in our sexual relationship.

☐ I feel my sexual needs are being met.

☐ I've told my wife what feels good and what I enjoy in our sexual relationship.

☐ My wife is not as interested in sex as I am.

☐ I struggle with pornography.

☐ Sex is boring; I'd like to try new things, but I'm embarrassed to ask my wife.

☐ My wife has difficulty reaching orgasm.

☐ We are so busy that sex is usually rushed.

☐ I am often too tired for sex.

☐ Sometimes I don't feel sexually confident with my wife.

How would you rate your sexual relationship with your wife? (circle one)

Non-Existent 0/10

Disappointing 1/10

Boring 2/10

Take it or Leave it 3/10

Sub-Standard 4/10

Adequate 5/10

Improving 6/10

Pleasurable 7/10

In a Good Place 8/10

Almost Perfect........................ 9/10

In Heaven!............................ 10/10

On average, how often do you and your wife have sex? (circle one)

Frequently - At least once a day!

Regularly - Several times per week

Routinely - Once per week

Occasionally - two or three times per month

Seldom - Less than once per month

Rarely - We go without sex for months at a time

How often would you like to have sex with your wife? (circle one)

Frequently - At least once a day!

Regularly - Several times per week

Routinely - Once per week

Occasionally - two or three times per month

Seldom - Less than once per month

HER INTIMACY SURVEY

Check all of the following statements that apply to you:

☐ My husband and I are comfortable talking about sex.

☐ We laugh and have fun during sex.

☐ My husband and I know where to find the female g-spot.

☐ Our sex life has improved in the past year.

☐ My husband and I kiss more now than in our first year of marriage.

☐ I initiate sex at least 25% of the time.

☐ We try to include variety in our sexual relationship.

☐ I feel my sexual needs are being met.

☐ I've told my husband what feels good and what I enjoy in our sexual relationship.

☐ My husband is not as interested in sex as I am.

☐ I struggle with pornography.

☐ Sex is boring; I'd like to try new things, but I'm embarrassed to ask my husband.

☐ My husband has difficulty reaching orgasm.

☐ We are so busy that sex is usually rushed.

☐ I am often too tired for sex.

☐ Sometimes I don't feel sexually confident with my husband.

How would you rate your sexual relationship with your husband? (circle one)

Non-Existent 0/10

Disappointing 1/10

Boring 2/10

Take it or Leave it 3/10

Sub-Standard 4/10

Adequate 5/10

Improving 6/10

Pleasurable 7/10

In a Good Place 8/10

Almost Perfect..................... 9/10

In Heaven!...................... 10/10

On average, how often do you and your husband have sex? (circle one)

Frequently - At least once a day!

Regularly - Several times per week

Routinely - Once per week

Occasionally - two or three times per month

Seldom - Less than once per month

Rarely - We go without sex for months at a time

How often would you like to have sex with your husband? (circle one)

Frequently - At least once a day!

Regularly - Several times per week

Routinely - Once per week

Occasionally - two or three times per month

Seldom - Less than once per month

INTIMACY QUESTIONS TO ASK YOUR PARTNER

For this next assignment, we recommend you go out for a leisurely walk or a romantic dinner with your spouse. Take the opportunity during your "date" to ask each other the following questions related to sexual intimacy in your relationship. Remember: you're NOT asking these questions to interrogate your partner, but to better understand them and deepen intimacy in your marriage! (Hint: Don't ask these questions on the same day you complete and discuss the "Intimacy Survey". You might find that too intense!)

It is important to remember that this could be a tough assignment. Make sure you are open to hear, and are supportive and caring in your responses!

INTIMACY QUESTIONS

1. Were sex and sexuality spoken about candidly in your family when you were growing up? How do you think this has affected our marriage?

2. Why might it be difficult for us to talk openly about sex?

3. What "emotional baggage" about sex might you be carrying:

   - because of your upbringing?
   - because of previous relationships?
   - because you've experienced sexual abuse?
   - because of pre-marital sexual experiences?
   - because of struggling with pornography or impure thoughts?

   Would it be helpful for us to see a counselor about any of these circumstances?

4. What can we do together to educate ourselves about and/or improve our sex life?

SEX CHALLENGE PRE-READING: LAYING THE FOUNDATION FOR SEVEN DAYS OF SEX

Before the actual seven-day period begins, let's work through the six concepts critical for success in this challenge. They'll help you understand your spouse, develop new, healthy habits, and discover new relationship skills.

The six concepts are:
- The Truth about Commitment
- The Truth about Forgiveness
- The Truth about Design
- The Truth about Vows
- The Truth about Rewinding
- The Truth about Sex

WHAT IS INTIMACY?

We've all heard that the tip of an iceberg (the part we see above the surface of the water) is only about 10% of the entire structure. What lies beneath the surface of the water is massive compared to what is visible to the eye! In the same way, what is under the surface in your relationship makes all the difference.

Below the surface of all fulfilling sexual relationships are authentic emotional, intellectual, and spiritual connections. Sex is just the tip of the intimacy iceberg!

Four Types of Intimacy

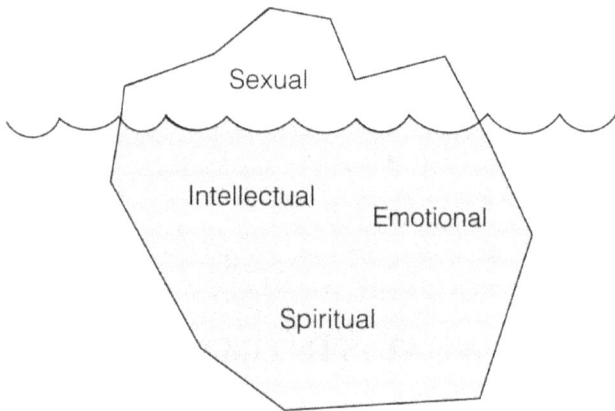

Sexual

Intellectual   Emotional

Spiritual

1. Sexual Intimacy

Most forms of intimacy can be experienced between any two people; however, it is sexual intimacy, reserved between husband and wife, that makes marriage the most unique of all relationships. In sex, a man and wife are made one flesh (Genesis 2:24).

2. Emotional Intimacy

It's in this particular area of closeness that romance best fits into the picture. When our emotions are involved, things get very interesting!

It's all the warm, cozy feelings of falling in love and being in love that we think of when we consider emotional intimacy.

All the words, thoughts, and actions that affect how we feel about our spouse and our marriage have a bearing on emotional intimacy. What is the best word to use? Romance!

3. Intellectual Intimacy

Intellectual intimacy is perhaps the most overlooked form of intimacy. Nevertheless, it is this intellectual closeness that often first connects two people together. Granted, a man may be attracted by the physical appearance of a woman, but it is the closeness developed through getting to know each other intellectually that initially draws a couple to each other.

Consider this example: *April and Doug are deeply in love with each other but they seem oddly matched. Doug is a big outgoing guy from rural Canada and April is a very shy, petite girl from Southeastern Asia. Doug and April met online, and began a courtship in cyberspace.*

How can a relationship like Doug and April's work? It can work because falling in love is often started by developing intellectual intimacy!

Many couples feel that spark of excitement growing between them as they spend time conversing and getting to know each other. This process begins intellectually and quickly becomes emotional as well.

4. Spiritual Intimacy

Based on the bedrock of common values and beliefs, spiritual intimacy extends our oneness to the very core of who we are, and influences how we perceive ourselves and the world around us.

Arguably the most neglected intimacy, spiritual intimacy is also the most important, because it is a tri-intimacy involving husband, wife, and God. Our relationship with God is like the hub of a wheel. Everything else in life comes into balance when the Lord has the central position in our marriage.

In our marriage vows, husband and wife make a vow to each other and also to God. Our vows include Him. With this understanding, as we grow closer to our spouse spiritually, we also grow closer to God. That's what this seven-day challenge is really about—deeper intimacy.

The pursuit of increased intimacy is a life-long journey, but in these next seven days, you will practice things that will change how you think, behave, and act. *You* need to change. Remember, work on yourself—don't try to work on your spouse!

THE TRUTH ABOUT COMMITMENT

In our present western culture, a long-lasting marriage is becoming increasingly less-common. With over thirty-two years of marriage behind us, we're convinced that a happy marriage of many years is more likely to occur between couples who are committed not only to one another and their marriage, but also to Jesus Christ. The building blocks of marriage success are the very values and perspectives that true Christianity produces!

In an article by Dr. Greg Swenson, a study of 351 couples experiencing longevity in their marriages for more than fifteen years is cited[1]. Respondents were asked to choose reasons for their long-lasting marriage. The top seven reasons were ranked in the following order:

1. My spouse is my best friend.

2. I like my spouse as a person.

3. Marriage is a long-term commitment.

4. Marriage is sacred.

5. We agree on aims and goals.

6. My spouse has grown more interesting.

7. I want the relationship to succeed.

Besides the rather amazing fact that husbands and wives cumulatively agreed on the rank order of the first seven reasons, we find it interesting that three of the seven reasons are directly related to the idea of *commitment*. Three others, including the first two, focus on the *value* of the other person as an individual.

---

[1] "What is the Answer to the Marriage Dilemma?" Greg Swenson, accessed March 29, 2015, http://www.gregswensonphd.com/aboutmarriage.htm.

Not surprisingly, commitment and valuing spouse over self are also some of the raw materials of intimacy. No one said a lasting marriage is easy; it's not! However, when people are willing to make changes in attitude and action, the results can be positively staggering! What is this willingness? We call it commitment!

We have asked both you and your spouse to make a commitment to this *7-Day Sex Challenge*. That commitment means you promise each other that you will fulfill the elements listed for each of the seven days.

The *7-Day Sex Challenge* requires vulnerability from both of you. Vulnerability only happens when there is trust. When your spouse knows you are committed to completing the challenge, they are able to have trust leading to vulnerability.

The *7-Day Sex Challenge* is not an empty promise or untested theory. It will really work for you if you commit to following it through for seven days!

THE TRUTH ABOUT FORGIVENESS

Ruth Bell Graham (wife of Rev. Billy Graham) said, "A happy marriage is the union of two good forgivers." Forgiveness is the act and (sometimes repetitive) process of letting go of the hurt and resentment of an offence. It happens when:

- We release the person who hurt us to God's care and concern.

- We let God take care of whatever He wants to do with the offence and the offender.

- We surrender our right and expectation for the offender to either apologize or be punished somehow for their wrong.

In every marriage, partners hurt each other, sometimes deeply. We must forgive.

The world-famous Mayo Clinic has identified the medical benefits of forgiveness.[2]

Researchers have recently become interested in studying the effects of forgiveness and unforgiveness. Evidence is mounting that holding on to grudges and bitterness results in long-term health problems. Forgiveness, on the other hand, offers numerous benefits, including:

- Lower blood pressure
- Stress reduction
- Less hostility
- Better anger management skills
- Lower heart rate
- Lower risk of alcohol or substance abuse
- Fewer depression symptoms
- Fewer anxiety symptoms
- Reduction in chronic pain
- More friendships
- Healthier relationships

---

[2] "Forgiveness: Letting Go of Grudges and Bitterness," Mayo Clinic, accessed March 29, 2015, http://www.mayoclinic.org/healthy-living/adult-health/in-depth/forgiveness/art-20047692.

- Greater religious or spiritual well-being
- Improved psychological well-being

Forgiving Others Sets Us Free

For your marriage to go to the next level, you must forgive. This can be extremely difficult for some: but there are no other options! To nurse a grudge and harbour bitterness will destroy your marriage and your health! Forgiving others actually sets us free!

It is very interesting that Jesus told us we had to forgive in the Lord's Prayer:

Our Father in Heaven,
Hallowed be Your name.
Your Kingdom come.
Your will be done on earth as it is in heaven.
Give us this day our daily bread.
And forgive us our debts, as we forgive our debtors.
And do not lead us into temptation, but deliver us
from the evil one.
For Yours is the kingdom and the power and the glory
forever. Amen. (Matthew 6:6-8)

And then, Jesus goes on to say, *"If you forgive those*

who sin against you, your heavenly Father will forgive you. But if you refuse to forgive others, your Father will not forgive your sin" (Matthew 6:14-15). A casual reader might get the mistaken idea that Jesus is demanding we earn His forgiveness through forgiving others—doing our part, so to speak. Is He really telling us that if we fail to forgive others, we have failed to do our part and we will not be forgiven ourselves?

Actually, no! Quite the opposite...

Jesus is telling us that if we fail to forgive others who have hurt and wounded us, our hearts will be contaminated with bitterness and resentment. We will automatically erect emotional walls within our hearts to prevent people from getting too close, and hurting us all over again. With these walls and bitterness, even God's love cannot break in!

On the other hand, when we learn to forgive others, we prevent those huge emotional walls from rising up, and our hearts stay soft and free from bitterness. Then, God's forgiveness is also able to get in!

We have witnessed couples forgive each other for past offences and sins that might have destroyed their marriages. When they did, they were free to emotionally move on in their relationships. Of course, it took some time for trust to be built up again, but their marriages were heading in the right direction!

THE TRUTH ABOUT DESIGN

God's design for marriage is found in Ephesians 5:22-33. This design follows a pattern of love and respect. A woman is to respect her husband because respect is fundamental to his needs. A man, on the other hand, must love his wife because love is fundamental to her needs.

Wives, understand and support your husbands in ways that show your support for Christ. The husband provides leadership to his wife the way Christ does to his church, not by domineering but by cherishing. So just as the church submits to Christ as he exercises such leadership, wives should likewise submit to their husbands.

Husbands, go all out in your love for your wives, exactly as Christ did for the church—a love marked by giving, not getting. Christ's love makes the church whole. His words evoke her beauty. Everything he does and says is designed to bring the best out of her, dressing her in dazzling white silk, radiant with holiness. And that is how husbands ought to love their wives. They're really doing themselves a favour since they're already "one" in marriage.

No one abuses his own body, does he? No, he feeds and pampers it. That's how Christ treats us, the church, since we are part of his body. And this is why a man leaves father and mother and cherishes his wife. No longer two, they become "one flesh." This is a huge mystery, and I don't pretend to understand it all. What is clearest to me is the way Christ treats the church. And this provides a good picture of how each husband is to treat his wife, loving himself in loving her, and how each wife is to honour her husband. (Ephesians 5:22-33 The Message)

In the middle of conflict, couples tend to fixate on the offence of their spouse. We are experts at defending and justifying ourselves, and putting the blame where we think it really belongs… at the feet of our spouse! This approach never works. Instead, the Lord taught us to forgive, and then meet the needs of our spouse.

Husbands, love like Jesus loved. He gave Himself without reservation, even though no one appreciated or valued His personal sacrifice. How can you practically make your wife feel cherished and loved? Doing this will require you to sacrifice your own desires, pleasures, or plans.

Wives, respect and submit like the church does to Jesus. How can you show your husband an attitude of submission and respect? Doing this requires you to value your husband's thoughts and ideas, to appreciate him, and to be supportive of him.

Wives, you might be thinking, "But he might take advantage of me!" And, of course, husbands may also be thinking along similar lines. To both nervous wives and husbands, we say, "Yes, that is a possibility! That's why we need commitment...and that's why we need to remember God's design!" As part of the commitment for the *7-Day Sex Challenge* you'll read to one another a "Statement of Biblical Design for Marriage" based on Ephesians 5.

THE TRUTH ABOUT VOWS

We believe couples need to make a big deal about their vows.

A vow is a solemn promise before God that must not be broken. In marriage, it is the ultimate act of commitment between two people. Consider the strength of the following vow I (Jim) have made to Carrie:

Carrie, I affirm and recommit to the vows I spoke to you on our wedding day: I will remain your faithful partner in life during sickness and in health, in our good times and in bad, throughout our joys and our sorrows.

Carrie, I vow to love you unconditionally, support you in your goals, honour and respect you, laugh with you and cry with you, and cherish you as long as we both shall live.

As couples, we need to be reminded about the promises we made to each other!

Some people enter into marriage thinking, "If this doesn't work out, I can always get a divorce and start over again." What is the devastating reality of divorce? If divorce is an option in people's minds, they tend to default to this easy-out in the face of serious marriage trouble.

Over the years, we've seen this tragic scenario play out with numerous couples who did not take their vows seriously.

For each day of the *7-Day Sex Challenge*, part of your homework will be to read marriage vows to each other, as well as statements about loving and respecting one another in accordance with God's design for marriage.

THE TRUTH ABOUT REWINDING

Rewinding is going back to treat your husband/wife as you did when you were first married. It's rewinding your life, remembering the excitement and how you spent so much time talking, laughing, or simply looking at each other!

The Bible refers to a group of people who, at one time, loved God with all their heart; but over time, they allowed that love to slip away. Finally, the Lord called these people to repentance. Repentance means to change your thinking.

Think about this: God told them, *"You have left your first love. Repent [change your thinking] and remember from where you have fallen. Return and do the things you used to do"* (Revelation 2:4-5 NAS[3]). God's call was for this particular church to rewind, go back and do what they used to do, act like they used to act, and talk like they used to talk when they were still in love with God!

Do you still write love notes to your husband or wife? When was the last time you called your spouse in the middle of the day to tell them you're thinking of them, and you love them?

Husbands, do you surprise your wife with flowers or small gifts regularly? Or do you only do the predictable things on birthdays or anniversaries?

Wives, when was the last time you met your husband at the bedroom door in lacy lingerie?

Husbands, when was the last time you told your wife you would do the supper dishes and get the children into bed, so she could put her feet up and relax? (That is romance at its best!)

At the beginning, when romantic love was fresh, we would do crazy things because of our love. Let's

---

[3]   New American Standard Bible

rewind and start doing some of those same crazy things again!

THE TRUTH ABOUT SEX

No matter where your marriage relationship is right now, the sizzle and spark can be restored! It doesn't have to take years: it can take just seven days!

Marriage is the only relationship on earth that provides everything necessary for awesome, sizzling sex! Every other type of relationship—casual sex, living together, or any other arrangement—just does not work! Oh, there may be excitement for a time but that time is short, and the painful consequences of sex outside of marriage are horrendous.

Sex is like our marriage's thermometer. It is a pretty accurate indicator of the health of the relationship. When our marriage is having trouble, then satisfying, exciting sex is the first thing to go! On the other hand, a dynamic, sizzling sex life is a pretty good indication that husband and wife are talking, laughing, communicating, and loving each other!

But even sex can become routine, predictable, and boring. Putting the spark back into sex may require trying new things, in new places, at new times!

Here is a list of suggestions for adding sizzle.

Foreplay

Spend more time focusing on the wife. Massaging, kissing, caressing, and playing should be carried on for a minimum of twenty minutes. Try keeping your clothes on for most of that time! You may be surprised at the arousal this brings!

Try Something New...Oral Sex

Trying new things will spice up sex amazingly! Talk openly with your spouse about desires, thoughts, inhibitions, and godly morality. You may be surprised at what the Bible says about sex ("Christian Views on Sex" on page 123).

Talk to Each Other

Sex starts in the brain; in our thinking! Because of this, there is nothing more intimate and sexually exciting than for a couple to talk to each other candidly, openly, and lovingly about what they would like to do to make their partner feel loved, excited, and sexually fulfilled! Being vulnerable and open is what intimacy is all about! That includes how you're feeling and what you would like to feel!

The only way for your marriage to improve is to do things differently than you are doing right now! What you do is determined by what you believe which, in turn, is determined by what you think. Therefore, you must:

- Change what you think.
- Change what you believe.
- Change what you do.

DEALING WITH ROADBLOCKS

Whether you're beginning the *7-Day Sex Challenge* with a healthy marriage relationship or not, there are no guarantees that you and your spouse will find it easy to complete the various parts of the challenge every day for seven days. There could be many reasons...

- Your planned time for sex is taken up with an unexpected circumstance
- You and/or your spouse are facing a difficult situation and lose all motivation to participate in the challenge
- One of you is unwell
- One of your kids is unwell

- The two of you become emotionally disconnected from one another through a misunderstanding
- You had an argument that doesn't get resolved
- You are both too tired
- and the list goes on!

If this happens to you, please don't give up! Instead, continue using the *7-Day Sex Challenge* as a tool to keep the two of you talking about what is best for your relationship.

Know that it's okay for you and your spouse to decide to skip a day of having sex. You both are to be commended for taking time to work on your relationship, even if you don't complete the *Sex Challenge* for the entire seven days! An argument, hurt, or disappointment with your spouse is difficult to work through; use the resources of the *7-Day Sex Challenge* to help you both get back on track and reconnect with one another.

Remember, the goal of the *7-Day Sex Challenge* is to reach the next level of intimacy, joy, and sexual fulfillment! May you have success in finishing the *7-Day Sex Challenge*, but more importantly, success in your relationship!

Part 2

The

Challenge!

STATEMENT OF BIBLICAL DESIGN FOR MARRIAGE

Ask the Lord Jesus to help you implement these important statements into your habits and perspective. Then,

1. Take time each morning of the seven days to read your section of God's Design for Marriage to your spouse.

2. Be sure to hold hands and look into your spouse's eyes as you read.

3. Tenderly kiss your spouse after you've read your section.

This statement is adapted from the popular marriage text in Ephesians 5 and 1 Corinthians 13, the "Love Chapter," in the New Testament of the Bible. (For more information, review the chapter on "The Truth about Design" on page 47.)

FOR THE HUSBAND

Read this to your wife while holding her hand and looking into her eyes:

I recognize that God's design for me is to love you in the same way Jesus loved the church. I need to love you more than I love myself.

The love God describes:

- *is patient and kind*
- *is not boastful or envious*
- *is not jealous or rude*
- *does not demand its own way*
- *is not irritable*
- *seeks to cherish*

With the Lord helping me, I will demonstrate this type of love today!

(Don't forget to kiss her gently!)

FOR THE WIFE

Read this to your husband while holding his hand and looking into his eyes:

I recognize that God's design for me is to respect you in the same way the church honours Jesus. I need to love you more than myself.

Honouring you in this way involves:

- *encouraging, not complaining*
- *helping, not challenging*
- *respecting, not demeaning*
- *trusting, not nagging*
- *giving, not withholding*
- *submitting, not controlling*

With the Lord helping me, I will demonstrate this type of honour today!

(Don't forget to kiss him gently!)

MARRIAGE VOWS

The vows you spoke to one other, and before God, when you were married may be somewhat different from the vows included here. Nevertheless, the main elements will be the same.

For each of the seven days, repeat your vows to one another as a reminder of your promises. Husbands, we suggest you do this first; then the wives repeat the vows.

MARRIAGE VOWS

(Spouse's name), I affirm and recommit to the vows I spoke to you on our wedding day:

- *I will remain your faithful partner in life*
- *during sickness and in health*
- *in our good times and in bad*
- *throughout our joys and our sorrows*

I vow to:

- *love you unconditionally*
- *support you in your goals*
- *honour and respect you*
- *laugh with you and cry with you, and*
- *cherish you as long as we both shall live*

SIMPLE SEX-GESTIONS

Variety, exploration, fun, and adventure are all part of the *7-Day Sex Challenge*!

We have included this list of suggestions—sex-gestions—for you to use. Feel free to add your own ideas! Choose at least three of these to use during the seven days.

Here's another thought: why don't you and your spouse take turns choosing one "sex-gestion" from the list each day?

- Write a sexy love letter to your spouse
- Offer oral sex
- Set out scented candles in the bedroom

- Try a new position for intercourse
- Put romantic music on
- Have sex in a different room of the house
- Extend foreplay with your clothes on as long as you can
- Offer to give your spouse a massage
- Make an appointment with your spouse for sex in the middle of the day
- Use whipping cream and/or chocolate syrup creatively during foreplay
- Start with a slow dance to your favourite love song
- Turn off all electronic devices (phones, computers, televisions, etc.) during lovemaking
- Purchase lubricant that gives a tingly sensation
- Put fresh linen on your bed
- Tell your spouse a sexual fantasy about the two of you
- Go to bed naked
- Call your spouse during the day to say you are looking forward to sex later

Day
1

HIS DAY ONE JOURNAL

Date: _____

- Read Biblical Design for Marriage

- Read Marriage Vows

- Bring Your Wife to Orgasm

- Write in Your Journal

My thoughts and observations:

_____

_____

_____

_____

_____

_____

_____

_____

_____

_____

_____

_____

_____

HER DAY ONE JOURNAL

Date: _____

- Read Biblical Design for Marriage

- Read Marriage Vows

- Bring Your Husband to Orgasm

- Write in Your Journal

My thoughts and observations:

_____

_____

_____

_____

_____

_____

_____

_____

_____

_____

_____

_____

HIS DAY TWO JOURNAL

Date: _____

- Read Biblical Design for Marriage

- Read Marriage Vows

- Bring Your Wife to Orgasm

- Write in Your Journal

My thoughts and observations:

_____

_____

_____

_____

_____

_____

_____

_____

_____

_____

_____

_____

HER DAY TWO JOURNAL

Date: _____

- Read Biblical Design for Marriage

- Read Marriage Vows

- Bring Your Husband to Orgasm

- Write in Your Journal

My thoughts and observations:

_____

_____

_____

_____

_____

_____

_____

_____

_____

_____

_____

_____

_____

Day

3

HIS DAY THREE JOURNAL

Date: _____

- Read Biblical Design for Marriage

- Read Marriage Vows

- Bring Your Wife to Orgasm

- Write in Your Journal

My thoughts and observations:

_____

_____

_____

_____

_____

_____

_____

_____

_____

_____

_____

_____

_____

HER DAY THREE JOURNAL

Date: _____

- Read Biblical Design for Marriage

- Read Marriage Vows

- Bring Your Husband to Orgasm

- Write in Your Journal

My thoughts and observations:

_____

_____

_____

_____

_____

_____

_____

_____

_____

_____

_____

_____

_____

Day

4

HIS DAY FOUR JOURNAL

Date: _____

- Read Biblical Design for Marriage

- Read Marriage Vows

- Bring Your Wife to Orgasm

- Write in Your Journal

My thoughts and observations:

_____

_____

_____

_____

_____

_____

_____

_____

_____

_____

_____

_____

_____

HER DAY FOUR JOURNAL

Date: _____

- Read Biblical Design for Marriage

- Read Marriage Vows

- Bring Your Husband to Orgasm

- Write in Your Journal

My thoughts and observations:

_____

_____

_____

_____

_____

_____

_____

_____

_____

_____

_____

_____

_____

Day
5

HIS DAY FIVE JOURNAL

Date: _____

- Read Biblical Design for Marriage

- Read Marriage Vows

- Bring Your Wife to Orgasm

- Write in Your Journal

My thoughts and observations:

_____

_____

_____

_____

_____

_____

_____

_____

_____

_____

_____

_____

HER DAY FIVE JOURNAL

Date: _____

- Read Biblical Design for Marriage

- Read Marriage Vows

- Bring Your Husband to Orgasm

- Write in Your Journal

My thoughts and observations:

_____

_____

_____

_____

_____

_____

_____

_____

_____

_____

_____

_____

_____

_____

Day

6

HIS DAY SIX JOURNAL

Date: _____

- Read Biblical Design for Marriage

- Read Marriage Vows

- Bring Your Wife to Orgasm

- Write in Your Journal

My thoughts and observations:

_____

_____

_____

_____

_____

_____

_____

_____

_____

_____

_____

_____

_____

HER DAY SIX JOURNAL

Date: _____

- Read Biblical Design for Marriage

- Read Marriage Vows

- Bring Your Husband to Orgasm

- Write in Your Journal

My thoughts and observations:

_____

_____

_____

_____

_____

_____

_____

_____

_____

_____

_____

_____

_____

_____

Day
7

HIS DAY SEVEN JOURNAL

Date: _____

- Read Biblical Design for Marriage

- Read Marriage Vows

- Bring Your Wife to Orgasm

- Write in Your Journal

My thoughts and observations:

_____

_____

_____

_____

_____

_____

_____

_____

_____

_____

_____

_____

_____

HER DAY SEVEN JOURNAL

Date: _____

- Read Biblical Design for Marriage

- Read Marriage Vows

- Bring Your Husband to Orgasm

- Write in Your Journal

My thoughts and observations:

_____

_____

_____

_____

_____

_____

_____

_____

_____

_____

_____

_____

_____

_____

AFTER GLOW

You made it! Your *7-Day Sex Challenge* is over! Now let's discover what's changed. Use the following questions as discussion starters with your spouse.

1. You committed to completing this week-long marriage adventure. What were some of the obstacles you encountered? How were you able to overcome them?
2. Assuming you had not repeated your vows since your wedding day, talk about your experiences saying them this week.
3. Did you learn something new about your spouse this past week?

4. Did the extra time and focus on sex enrich the experience?
5. Did you try a sex-gestion that worked really well?
6. Do you think your love-making has improved?
7. Did you have fun?!

We wish you and your spouse all the best as you continue in your new, more intimate relationship. The time and effort you've invested will pay off! It did for us!

Blessings to both of you!

Jim and Carrie

Bonus Challenge

Why not commit to doing the *7-Day Sex Challenge* again sometime? Though it takes effort to keep the commitments of the *Sex Challenge* every day for seven days, your marriage will benefit any time you invest and work at improving it.

We suggest doing the *7-Day Sex Challenge* once or twice each year. Are you up for it?

Additional Resources

CHRISTIAN VIEWS ON SEX

Christian views on sex are varied and extreme! What we must be careful to discern is the difference between what the Bible actually says about sex and sexuality, and what our particular background and upbringing may teach us.

How Do We Know What's Okay?!

Wouldn't it be nice to have a list of sexual practices categorized by "sinful" or "okay"? Is there such a list? Would everyone agree with the list? Is there a solution to this dilemma?

We think the answers to those questions are: yes, no, no, and probably not in that order. — Melissa and Louis McBurney, M.D.

Believe us when we say there are many different Christian views on sex and sexual practices and on what is Biblically acceptable! As stated in the above quote, we are not going to find a complete list. What we will find, however, are commands from God's Word—let's call them "Thou Shalt Nots"; as well as principles that are universally true in their application, and can be used by individual couples to help them decide their own views.

Thou Shalt Nots: Commands!

Christian views on sex must be formed by what the Bible says. The Bible is very straightforward regarding certain prohibitions that, if obeyed, place a clear fence of protection around the marriage union and the sanctity of God's design for sexuality between a husband and wife. Let's take a look at them.

God plainly forbids adultery (having sex with someone other than your spouse) and calls it sin. The Bible forbids fornication (sexual promiscuity or having sex outside of marriage) as sinful as well.

God's prohibitions to us are not intended as limitations to our freedom; they are protections to our well-being. Slapping the hand of an infant reaching toward a hydro receptacle would not be called limiting the child's fun and curiosity. It would represent a responsible parent protecting her young child from certain injury! So it is with God's "Thou Shalt Nots". They protect us from certain moral, physical, and emotional danger.

In the Sermon on the Mount (Matthew 5,6,7), Jesus taught us that outward actions (like adultery and fornication) stem from an inner motivation of our heart. Jesus then showed us that lustful thoughts about a woman who is not your wife constituted adultery from God's perspective! Christian views on sex are not based on public opinion, but on God's Word.

Other sexual sins that are specifically listed in Scripture include homosexuality, bestiality, and incest (Leviticus 18, Romans 1:21-32, 1 Thessalonians 4:1-8, and 1 Corinthians 6:12-20).

The One and Only Principle refers to the sacred covenant between husband and wife that constitutes the bedrock of their relationship. Saying to your spouse, "You are my one and only love in this life!" develops trust and commitment. Since intimacy is the element that guarantees sexual satisfaction, it will not be developed unless a high degree of commitment is invested in the marriage. Unfaithfulness of any kind erodes this key element. Basically, the Christian views on sex are summed up with: one man and one woman, for life!

The Back to Basics Principle also reminds us of God's design in terms of the physiology of sex. God made husbands and wives to enjoy each other sexually! Check the plumbing, and you will discover that intercourse between the man's penis and the woman's vagina is the foundation of sex!

Whatever sexual practices couples may enjoy, the Back to Basics Principle reminds couples that genital union should be a regular part of lovemaking.

The Hooked on You Principle will force out of your life any form of sexuality or sensuality that is not directly targeted toward your spouse. Sex is a pleasure-bond that keeps a husband and wife close to each other. Anything they do, or anything they see that draws them away from each other, or makes them dependent on anything except their spouse, must be eliminated from their marriage!

Pornography, inappropriate sexual behaviours, online chat rooms, fetishes, immoral fantasies, or imaginations that become habit-forming draw couples away from each other.

The Good for Both Principle reminds us that every practice in a sexual relationship must be good for both spouses. Sex was meant to be fun and feel good for both husband and wife! If, for example, the husband wants to try something different during their lovemaking (let's say oral sex), but that isn't pleasurable for his wife, he needs to practice restraint and drop the request!

For this principle, conscience is a keyword. We should never expect our partner to violate their conscience.

The Give and Take Principle addresses the huge differences between the basic sexual wiring of men and woman. Some wives may be totally satisfied by hugging, snuggling, and enjoying romance with their husbands, and could even do without sex all together! For the basic needs of some women, sex may rank somewhere near #26, just after gardening! Men, well...they're different. Men's basic needs usually consist of air, food, and sex. Given the differing sexual desires and appetites between men and women, it follows that sex is often the cause of much friction in a marriage.

The solution to the differences is two-fold:

1. Focus on pleasing your spouse (the Good for Both Principle)

2. Practice compromising or giving in whenever you can to the desires of your spouse (the Give and Take Principle).

For example, let's say a wife's conscience is bothered by her husband's request for oral sex. The couple needs to determine if this is a matter of conscience because of her upbringing, or because of a biblical example or principle. The couple may discover that trying oral sex is not a moral or biblical issue, but a hesitation because of her background. If the couple agrees to try a compromise position, then some hesitation toward oral sex might be alleviated for the wife if her husband wore a condom.

Christian views on sex must be shaped by adherence to the clear biblical commands, as well as attention to the general principles present in the Bible. For every couple's unique situations, the principles of Give and Take must be balanced with Good for Both.

THE ART OF INTIMATE CONVERSATION

Love talk or intimate conversation involves each person connecting with the other on the deepest of levels, where true inner feelings, dreams, hurts, and fears can be shared. Intimate conversation is often experienced early on in a relationship or marriage when couples express high degrees of interest and value in each other. Sadly, over time, these investments in the relationship are often let go, and so love conversation diminishes.

When examining the impact of conversation in a marriage relationship, Dr. William Harley, author of *His Needs, Her Needs*, refers to "friends and enemies" of good conversation.

Friends of Intimate Conversation

- use conversation to learn and understand more about your spouse
- develop interest in your spouse's favourite topics of conversation
- balance conversation: both sides have to talk and listen!
- give undivided attention to each other by eliminating distractions like the television and computer. Focus on each other and communicate!

Enemies of Intimate Conversation

- forcing people to agree with you
- dwelling on mistakes, past and present
- using conversation to punish one another

Simply stated, intimacy is developed through conversation that can lead to an unusually high degree of satisfaction in marriage.

THE ART OF FOREPLAY

Although this may technically be the preparation phase of lovemaking, the art of foreplay shouldn't be underestimated; classically for women, it's the best part! It is here that intimacy is at a climax (pardon the pun!), and wives are most enjoying sexual closeness.

The importance of the art of foreplay is understood when men take time well beforehand to focus on building an atmosphere of rest, relaxation, and romance. Removing distractions, stresses, and interruptions allows the woman to enjoy intimacy—the key component of sex.

For a man, foreplay and lovemaking are opportunities to practice authentic care, focusing on his wife's pleasure. Men must spend quality time getting their wives prepared for sexual fulfillment.

Foreplay must begin long before you are actually in the bedroom. Everything from opening the car door for your wife, to surprising her with a romantic love letter, to getting up when she enters a room in a public setting, all help her feel cherished and romanced.

A few simple suggestions:

- Spend plenty of time kissing. First gently, and gradually more passionately.
- Kiss and embrace fully clothed, then undress slowly.
- Give at least fifteen minutes of time for foreplay. (You will find that your orgasms are more intense after this extended time of preparation for lovemaking!)

Just remember, the most beautiful experience on earth should not be rushed! Foreplay is meant to be fun, so take time and enjoy each other!

HOW TO FRENCH KISS

Learning how to French kiss provides an intimate, passionate kiss where partners use their tongues, lips, and mouths. Since God designed both the lips and tongue to be highly sensitive and packed with nerve endings, a couple learning how to French kiss will enjoy an exciting, sensual experience!

1. Prepare. Always make sure you have fresh breath, clean teeth, and have focused on personal hygiene.

2. Moisten Your Lips. Rubbing your tongue over your lips is enough but don't do it just before you kiss! Using lip balm would be helpful.

3. Tilt Your Head Slightly. As you approach one another for the actual kiss, avoid a nose-to-nose collision by slightly tilting your head to one side.

4. Begin With a Gentle Closed-Mouth Kiss. Slow and gentle are the operative words here! Don't rush, lunge, or attack! Using variations of soft, brief kisses, withdraw slightly and engage again somewhat tentatively. Closing your eyes as you begin kissing prevents your partner from having to look cross-eyed at you!

5. Begin Touching With Your Tongue. While kissing, open your lips slightly, and gently touch your partner's lips with your tongue, or tentatively slip the end of your tongue through your partner's lips. If your partner does not respond in similar fashion, or if they pull away slightly, you must save your French kissing for another time when your partner is more prepared.

6. Tongue Exploration. With the assurance that your spouse is enjoying French kissing, try opening your mouth wider and moving your tongue a little more into their mouth. The key is mutual exploration. What does your partner enjoy? Too much, too far, too fast, too wet are

all turn-offs that can make this type of open-mouth kissing unpleasant. Because this type of kissing produces a lot of saliva, remember to swallow occasionally.

7. Change Things Up. Using a variety of kissing techniques and being aware of your partner's responses are paramount. It's about having fun and developing intimacy with your husband or wife. There is no right or wrong! What's important is your partner's enjoyment.

8. Remember the Purpose. Mutual pleasure and the development of intimacy are the consequences, but the purpose is to bring pleasure to your partner. It is to demonstrate to your wife or husband that you cherish and honour them.

THE ABCS OF GIVING A FULL BODY MASSAGE

There are many benefits that come from a full-body massage! Stress causing muscle tension is relieved, and endorphins are released producing relaxation. These endorphins are the body's natural painkillers; at the same time, they alleviate muscle pain and play a role in stimulating muscle tone.

Massaging your spouse also:

- enhances the body's range of motion
- improves breathing
- improves your sense of health
- improves circulation

- accelerates healing
- is a wonderful preparation for sex
- helps the body release oxytocin (referred to as the *cuddling* or *love* hormone)

The development of intimacy through touch is profound; consequently, giving full body massages is a must for couples pursuing ever-increasing intimacy.

A - Atmosphere and Mood

Setting the right atmosphere and mood is crucial to promote relaxation. Consider the following:

- Set a comfortable room temperature and eliminate drafts.
- Remove potential distractions: turn off phones, pull the drapes, and take away possible irritations.
- Play soothing, romantic music.
- Dim lights and use lightly scented candles.

B - Basic Tools

Some basic tools for giving a massage include:

- A firm surface so the body's muscles can be

fully supported. Obviously, a massage table is ideal but using a firm bed or the floor with appropriate pillows or towels for comfort will also work.

- Towels. For head support, if necessary, or for warmth in the event of coolness or draft.
- Massage oils, lubricants, or lotions to apply for aiding a smooth glide. (Apply to your hands first to warm it up!) If your partner is averse to oils, use talcum powder.
- Time. Giving a full body massage cannot be rushed, and should be done slowly.

C - Central Technique

Where to Massage

Begin on the shoulders and work up to the neck. The area between shoulders and neck often requires rubbing and kneading; use your thumbs to help remove tension that often resides. Move down both arms to include massaging the hands.

When finished, return to the back and buttocks, and begin working the tops of the legs separately, kneading each one. Move to the calves, and then proceed down, spending lots of time on the feet.

Start with deep, slow pressure and move to the toes, being careful on the soles of the feet, and in between the toes.

How to Massage

Here are a few types of strokes and ideas to use depending on where you are massaging:

- Kneading: squeeze the skin and muscles firmly, gently, and rhythmically.
- Circling hands: applying oil when necessary, use your hands to make circular motions.
- Continuous touch: once you have started the full body massage, do not remove both hands at the same time; you will break the touch bond with your spouse.
- Pressure: focus on large muscle groups like shoulders, neck, back, and legs. Use firm and even pressure, though not too forceful.

Don't apply pressure directly to the spine. Don't pinch. Don't tickle. Remember to massage in a way you would want to be touched and, if your spouse falls asleep, congratulate yourself! You have given a wonderful massage!

FEMALE ORGASM 101

Focusing too hard on reaching orgasm may, in fact, be one of the main contributors to the elusive nature of the female orgasms! Worrying about performing produces a psychological pressure that hinders women from relaxing. Consequently, both husband and wife can become frustrated.

Sex needs to be an activity that is free of guilt, nagging thoughts from the past, and unspoken expectations that place husband and wife in a state of stress. A fixation or preoccupation with reaching an orgasm might place stress on the woman that results in her focusing on performance, rather than just enjoying the attention and affection of her lover.

A key element in a totally exhilarating and satisfying experience, for both partners, is a slow and deliberate period of foreplay, where lovers can tease, play, and entice one another! Remember, it's supposed to be fun! If you're worried about not climaxing, you're putting too much pressure on yourself and not approaching sex in a healthy manner.

The female body is a work of art. To fully appreciate male and female climaxes, we must understand the nature of intimacy, and the full range of its implications. Intimacy occurs on four separate yet related fronts: the intellect, the emotions, the spirit, and the body.

On each of these fronts, there are considerations that we call *The Four C's*:

1. Communication
2. Caring
3. Commitment
4. Common Values

In this way, orgasm is not simply a physiological

release of accumulated sexual tension; it is the natural conclusion to a sexual relationship marked by these four attributes.

Practical Tips

Don't make having an orgasm your goal. If you do, both you and your wife will begin lovemaking with this expectation set up that you are trying to reach. Instead, make the goal the experience of making your spouse feel cherished and loved.

Spend lots and lots of time on foreplay! (kissing, cuddling, touching, teasing... did we mention kissing?)

Women have two areas that provide sexual pleasure (erogenous zones): the clitoris and the vagina.

Clitoris: this is one of the two organs whose sole purpose is to provide sexual pleasure! The areas around the clitoris are highly sensitive; extended foreplay and then stimulation of this area will produce orgasms.

Vagina: the inner area of the vagina is the most sensitive. There is a spot that has caused some confusion over the years: the g-spot. The g-spot is a zone about two or three inches inside the vagina on the front wall, closest to the clitoris or pubic bone. When aroused, the area swells with blood and becomes rough and raised. This area responds to pressure (not touch), and so deep massaging is the best way to produce an orgasm.

LOCATE HER G-SPOT AND GIVE HER MORE PLEASURE

Husbands, learn how to locate your wife's g-spot and you may help her experience an intense feeling of sexual pleasure she's never felt before!

A German gynecologist, Ernest Grafenberg, described this area found in the female genitals in the 1940's. Over the years, it has been a rather hotly contested phenomenon. Many doctors doubted whether this elusive area even existed. Unlike a man's sexual organ that doubles as part of the elimination system, a woman's sexual organs (clitoris and g-spot) have no other function. In other words, God gave women these organs for one reason and one reason only—to provide sexual pleasure!

That being the case, isn't it interesting that sex is often thought of as being primarily for the husband's pleasure? Some people think wives just tolerate sex because they love their husbands and know how important sex is to them.

If you have had the idea that sexual enjoyment is only for men—you're very mistaken! In actual fact, God designed women to have a greater *orgasmic potential* than men!

How to Find the G-Spot

The g-spot becomes engorged with blood during foreplay and so appropriate time needs to be spent on foreplay. The area itself, sometimes referred to as the urethral sponge, or Skene's glands feels like a very subtle bump two or three inches inside the vagina, about one to two inches in diameter.

After much foreplay, the g-spot will be somewhat enlarged. Place your finger on your wife's g-spot and massage firmly, increasing pressure. This area does not respond to light touching but only to deep massage.

Some women experience a feeling of needing to urinate at this point. Allow the feeling to continue knowing that, as tension builds up, the feeling will diminish and disappear. Continued deep, hard massage may trigger a vaginal orgasm which is often accompanied by female ejaculation. Yes, female ejaculation!

If this g-spot orgasm doesn't easily happen, continue with clitoral stimulation. With the stimulation of the g-spot that has taken place, female ejaculation will likely still occur.

Female ejaculation is highly pleasurable and it is not urine that is being produced! After the contractions are over, the husband should wait twenty seconds or so, and then continue firm massaging of the g-spot to produce multiple orgasms!

Why not talk to your wife about trying to locate her g-spot tonight?

ORAL SEX

Is Oral Sex Okay?

We believe that oral sex between husband and wife is an acceptable way of expressing love for each other within marriage. In the Bible, the Song of Solomon is most frequently cited as an example of a scriptural reference to oral sex:

Like an apple tree among the trees of the forest, so is my beloved among the young men. In his shade I took great delight and sat down, and his fruit was sweet to my taste. (Song of Solomon 2:3)

While the previous passage refers to fellatio (oral sex on the husband), the following can be read as a metaphor for cunnilingus (oral sex on the wife):

Awake, O north wind, and come, wind of the south; make my garden breathe out fragrance, let its spices be wafted abroad. May my beloved come into his garden and eat its choice fruits! (Song of Solomon 4:16)

And again, the Song of Solomon urges lovers to eat and drink freely of one another's bodies:

I am come into my garden, my sister, my spouse: I have gathered my myrrh with my spice; I have eaten my honeycomb with my honey; I have drunk my wine with my milk: eat, O friends; drink, yea, drink abundantly, O beloved. (Song of Solomon 5:1)

This reading of the Scriptures portrays the act of oral sex as both natural, like eating, and a joyful expression of love, passion, and sexual sharing between a man and woman.

In marriage, oral sex is acceptable before God. There is no Scriptural reason why a husband and wife should not enjoy it.

All that being said, we'd like to make one additional comment: it is very important for a husband or wife to respect their spouse, especially in areas where a spouse may feel uncomfortable with a type of sexual practice. Oral sex may be one of those areas.

WOMEN, HAVE YOU LOST INTEREST IN SEX?

In all honesty, there are times when I (Carrie) have little to no interest in sex and I lack sexual confidence. It may be that:

- I have allowed myself to get overtired,
- I'm not feeling well,
- I'm discouraged about my body image, or
- I've experienced a disappointment.

Still, I know that my sexual relationship with my husband is so important. Not only does it fulfill a need Jim has, but it's also an important way that he and I connect physically and emotionally. Because I value God's design for sex in marriage, I have set out to increase my sexual confidence. As I do that, I discover that my interest in sex with my husband increases too!

If you have lost interest in sex, let me suggest you begin to use the following nine actions to gain back that lost interest!

Nine Actions to Gain Back Interest in Sex:

1. Initiate Sex Yourself
2. Prepare Yourself All Day
3. Kiss Passionately
4. Give Enough Time for Sex
5. Keep Your Thoughts on Topic
6. Be Aggressive
7. Try Something New
8. Ladies, Treat Your Husband
9. Educate Yourself

1. Initiate Sex Yourself

Most women expect that if the husband wants sex, he will take the lead. Most husbands admit they can be more aroused when their wives initiate sex. It's amazing, ladies, when you initiate sex with your husband, you will gain sexual confidence and desire yourself!

2. Prepare Yourself All Day

Playful hugs, lingering kisses, loving phone calls or texts are just a few simple ways to help you prepare yourself—and your husband—for a passionate time of sex later in the day.

3. Kiss Passionately

Don't pass up the best way to increase passion and sexual desire. Be sure to communicate your love in this very basic but very powerful expression. Spend time embracing and kissing with lots of passion!

4. Give Enough Time for Sex

Make sure there is plenty of time for foreplay. Running out of time or having to finish sex in a rush is a sure way to diminish sexual desire.

5. Keep Your Thoughts on Topic!

Don't let yourself get distracted by what you need to do after sex (laundry, kids, work...). Whisper loving thoughts to your husband to help keep your mind involved with your love-making. Be creative and tell him a sexual fantasy about the two of you. This gives new meaning to "bedtime story"!

6. Be Aggressive

Rid yourself of inhibitions and be the aggressive sexual partner once in a while! Your husband will probably be aroused by your boldness. Don't allow yourself to be too relaxed; stay present and aware, or you may fall asleep before sex is done!

7. Try Something New

Try a new position, a new location, new lingerie, or a new time of day. Don't let your times of intimacy be predictable or boring. Keep them hot!

8. Ladies, Treat Your Husband

Find out what especially delights him and then do it! Become a student of your spouse and make it your goal to please him out of this world! The best sex is when we want to gratify our spouse more than ourselves.

9. Educate Yourself

Visit the bookstore or library or do some online research to find out how to have great sex! (Caution: Avoid the research whose content violates you and your spouse's moral values. Check the Resources section of our website for some good suggestions of books and websites.) Though there is some value to innocence and self-discovery, sometimes becoming educated will help you learn to overcome barriers to sex or learn how to enhance lovemaking.

Go for it, ladies! Don't wait for your lost interest in sex to come back on its own. Take steps to take it back and increase sexual desire!

ABOUT THE AUTHORS

Jim and Carrie Gordon, founders of The Intimate Couple website, are pastors, parents, and leaders who love to encourage couples in any way they can. They have nine children and nine grandchildren to-date, and have been married for thirty-three years. Jim and Carrie are proud to say they are more in love—and have better sex—now than ever before! They are passionate about helping other couples increase their marital intimacy to achieve the marriages of their dreams.